Here I Am Again, LORD!

Here I Am Again, Lord!

Betty Isler

Publishing House
St. Louis

Library of Congress Cataloging in Publication Data

Isler, Betty, 1915—
    Here I am again, Lord!

    1. Women—Prayer-books and devotions—English.
I. Title.
BV4844.I8   1983   242'.643   82-25273
ISBN 0-570-03895-2 (pbk.)

1 2 3 4 5 6 7 8 9 10   PP   92 91 90 89 88 87 86 85 84 83

Contents

OUTDOORS

AND ALL AROUND MY SOUL

MY WEEK

Indoors

Will I Ever Learn?

I am so old, Lord,
Still to be learning Your Word.
I read, I study, I listen.
One would think that
After all these years
At Your feet
I would have earned
A smidgeon of wisdom,
A certificate, perhaps.
At least a gold star.

But no!
Each day I find
There is still so much
I do not know,
So much yet to learn.
I am still at
First-grade level.

I guess that is why
You call me Your child.

Comfort

When I was little,
My mother would lay
The back of her hand
Against my cheek,
Feeling for fever.
That gesture alone
Was enough to comfort me,
To make me feel secure
And loved.

How often now,
In the deep, dark pocket
Of a sleepless night,
Have I felt Your hand
In just that way,
And felt secure
And loved.

Group Effort

Lord,
I think it was no accident
That You assembled this group
Of diverse personalities
For this committee.

You put us to the test,
Strained our patience,
Stretched our tolerance,
Shattered our self-images,
(I came home in tears one night,
Ready to resign.)

But You left us
One small piece
Of common ground.
There was work to be done,
Your work,
In Your name.

Now the task is completed
And everyone is smiling
And friendly.

Lord,
Were You showing us
One of Your miracles?

Hot Line

Telephone salesmen
Irritate me,
Calling at inconvenient times,
Invading my privacy,
Persisting with their pitch
Until I hang up.

Which reminds me
How often I dial YOU
At any hour,
Day or night,
And you never
Hang up.

Friend in Need

She is my best friend.
We support one another
At all times,
In all situations.
We share and we care.
We are so close.

But today
There is a distance
Between us,
A new tightness
In her voice
As she says,
"You simply do not understand
How it is for me!"

And she is so right, Lord,
Because, You see,
She is a new widow.

Please help her, Lord,
And help me, also,
To lend her strength,
Even when, by Your grace,
I do not know how it is.

Come, Lord Jesus

Lord,
Julia Child I am not.
I confess to a
Less than enthusiastic relationship
With pan and pot.

My cooking could possibly
Qualify my family
For passing
Survival training.

But Lord,
You have been our guest
At every single meal,
And I don't hear YOU
Complaining!

Teamwork

The task was so huge
I wilted before it.
I couldn't deliver the goods,
I swore it.
They must ask someone else,
That was all there was to it,
But I asked You for help,
And found WE could do it!

Appointment

There are days, Lord,
When I get up
To situations I cannot face.
When I draw the drapes
Against the light,
Ignore telephone
And door.
Shut myself away
From the day.

I need unbroken silence,
The calm of solitude,
A few hours in which
To sort out the confusions
Churning in my mind.

What I seek
Is a private conference
With You.

Thank You, Lord,
For always having time for me
On Your calendar.

Sick Call

Lord, I am so grateful
That as the Great Physician
You are always willing
To make house calls.

I would never make it
If You kept
Office hours.

The *Register* Regrets

How often, in the local press,
Have I found that tiny item
On an inside page,
The printed retraction
Of an earlier story
That was wrong . . .
The ineffective correction
After a man's name
Has been smeared,
Or a family disrupted,
A business destroyed
By careless reporting
Or proofreading.

Lord, help me to edit
The words of my mouth,
So that they do not injure
Or cause distress.
Help me to report
Only Your truths.

Assignment

Let's face it, Lord.
I'm in over my head
This time around.

I don't have the know-how,
Don't have the skill,
Don't have the ability,
Don't have the background.
I don't even know
Where to start.
They could have asked
Mickey Mouse and been
Farther ahead.
But they asked me!

So here I am again, Lord,
Floundering offshore,
Calling to my Lifesaver,
Help me, once more!

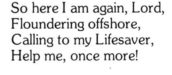

Do, Re, Thee

Lord,
You have given me a tin ear.
Let us say
Music is not my major.
I would not be welcome
In the choir.

I sing in the cracks,
My pitch
Is so off key
The folks in the pew ahead
Turn and look at me.

But I don't care!
Lord, I'm right in there
When it comes to
Singing Your praise.
THAT tune I can carry
For the rest of my days!

Waiting Room

He's in there, Lord,
Behind those heavy doors
Marked X-ray.

I'm out here, Lord,
With the green plastic chairs
And the green plastic palms
And the torn magazines,
And the clock
With the slow-moving hand.

He's in there,
Being scanned,
I'm out here,
Knowing You stand
Beside both of us.

Market Line

Lord,
You are so tolerant
When I come rushing to You
With my suddenly urgent
List of needs.

You let me through
The express lane
And never even count
The items.

Putting My House in Order

It is all very well
For me to make
A good impression:
Beds made, dishes done,
Everything polished
To Perfection.

It's what lurks
In the dark corners of my mind
That concerns me.
Those closet doors
Behind which I have piled
Prejudices and old hurts,
Grudges and small
Dishonesties,
The unaired attic
Of negative memories
Over which I weep.

Lord, once for all,
Help me to make
A clean sweep.

Speaking Engagement

Lord,
What am I doing here,
Before all these people,
All those smiling,
Expectant faces,
All those pencils
Poised above notebooks
Waiting for me to say
Something memorable?

Lord,
What am I doing here?
My mind is a vacuum,
My tongue inoperable,
Like a puppet
Without its working hand.
Help me!

And of course, as always,
I open my mouth
And out come the words
I am supposed to say,
Because they are not mine,
But Yours.

Rest Home Visitation

Lord,
It is such a joy
To bring Your love,
Your comfort and balm
To those shut-in souls
Who are so sweet and receptive,
So uncomplaining and calm,
Smiling their thanks.
It is too easy to feel smug
About these once-a-week
"Good deeds."

But Lord,
There are the others—
The disoriented, the hostile,
The destructive,
With soiled clothing
And unpleasant breath.

Lord,
Help me to bring Your love
To the unlovely,
Who need it so much.

From My Rocking Chair

Lord,
Let me not complain
About this cane,
Utter no moans
About achey bones,
Nor snidely degrade
This hearing aid.

For I walk erect
With You by my side,
No pain then hampers
My confident stride,
And Oh! How clearly,
And perfectly
I hear Your words
When You speak to me!

Children's Program

Lord,
Forgive me if I boast a bit.
After all,
I can claim personal kinship
With two angels
And a shepherd
In this Christmas program,
And You know how it is
With grandmothers!

Knowing You as I do,
I am sure You don't mind
If I bask in this
Reflected limelight,
Or if I enthuse,
Even when
The littlest angel
Gets the giggles
And the shepherd wears
Beat-up tennis shoes.

Convalescence

I have been given
The white pill
To relax the nerves;
The pink capsule
To cancel the pain;
The blue tablet for this,
The yellow for that.

Lord,
Help me to dispense with
This rainbow of
Chemical crutches.
Restore me
With the unadulterated,
Shining purity
Of Your healing strength.

Quarters Only

Lord,
I grow so impatient
With this coin-operated world.
I seem always to be seeking
Something from a monster
Whose slotted jaws demand
A particular coin
I do not have.

But You, Lord,
Supply all our needs,
Great and small,
And ask only the coin
Of belief.

Congregation

I look around me and see
So many quiet souls
Who serve You without fanfare,
Who expect, and receive,
No acclaim;
Drawing no attention
To themselves, yet
Filling their days
With Your work,
Honoring Your name,
Serving on committees,
Taking their turn,
Visiting the sick,
Showing concern.

Surely they are among
The most blessed of us,
Who set such examples
For the rest of us.

Intensive Care

They let me see him, finally,
This good man of mine,
Propped up against
The white pillow,
His body connected
By wires and tubes
To humming instruments
And a monitor whose red tongue
Licked across the screen
In jagged movements.

He managed a grin,
His eyes telling me
What we both knew:
The most important connection,
The invisible one
That would pull him through,
Was his direct line
To You.

Thank You, Lord!

Alive and Well

When I was ill,
A friend thoughtfully
Brought me a prayer plant.

I am embarrassed that,
In spite of my care,
The leaves shriveled
And the plant has not
Survived.

But, Lord,
I am happy to report
That my prayer LIFE
Has thrived!

Workshop

I sit in awe
Of this professional woman
Who leads our discussion.

She is so learned,
So educated,
So solidly grounded in theology
She never seems to falter.

She has university degrees
And doctorates
Streaming like a banner
Behind her name.

She does not lack humility,
And I love her, respect her
And admire her.

I am also, (forgive me!)
Intimidated by her . . .

Until I remember
That even as one
Of Your slower students,
I have my own master's degree
As a C.O.G.*

* Child of God

Emergency Room

You were there, waiting for me,
Weren't You, Lord,
When they rolled me in,
Short of breath and scared?

You were there
Behind those ceiling lights,
The clicking monitors,
The bottles and tubes,
Needles, dials,
And voices.

And You were there,
Weren't You, Lord,
With Your arm across his shoulders,
When my husband leaned over me
And smiled?
(Oh! thank You, Lord,
For supporting him
When I could not!)

Did you know, Lord,
That I dreamed I was floating
Up to those white gates?
But they were locked
And I was too tired
To rattle them,
So I drifted back down.

But of course you knew,
Because I heard You say,
"Not yet."

At Last

There was so little of her left,
Finally, in that hospital bed,
My once-plump, cheerful mother,
Now only a fleshless frame
Beneath the sheet.

I kept the coma vigil
Alone in the coma silence,
All hospital sounds suspended
Beyond that closed door,
Waiting.

I prayed
"Please take her"
Again and
Again.

From somewhere
A cool, fresh current
Brushed my face.
I saw the single rose
On her bedstand
Soundlessly drop its petals,
And she was gone.

You were there.

Beloved Strangers

They are so
Laid back and cool,
These grandchildren of mine,
Now into their late teens.

Sometimes I wonder
What lies beneath
That unrevealing surface,
That exterior calm
They wear as tightly
As their jeans.

I cradled and tended them
As infants,
And watched them grow
Into strangers,
Loving them and praying.
As the twig is bent
So will they go.

Outdoors

... and the Little Hills Rejoice

It has been a long, wet winter, Lord,
And the earth is heavy.
The trees are black,
And the streets are grey.
Everything seems to sag,
Including my spirits.
My bones ache in the damp,
And my footsteps drag.

But today there was a crack of sun,
The tiniest promise,
And we drove out into the hills.
Oh! The green of them, Lord!
No artist could ever reach that green
On his palette.
God's Green, I call it,
That dries out the bones
And makes the heart sing.

How like You, Lord,
After winter,
To give us Spring!

Just Our Luck

We had snatched a few hours
For a trip into the desert,
Into those rocks and hills
Whose colors my husband loves
To capture on canvas,
But the weather was bad.
"Just our luck," we said.

It began to rain,
Just enough to spot the car
And smear the windshield.
Just our luck.

And instead of all gold and sienna,
The desert floor
Was a muddy yellow
And the cliffs were dull umber
And the palos verde dead grey.
A totally miserable day.
Just our luck.

But to the west
A slant of sun
Suddenly pierced
Those black clouds,
And a rainbow appeared
Against the rocks.
Not in the sky, Lord,
But on the rocks,
Reflected on their wet surface!

Truly, Lord, there is no limit
To Your artistry!

38

My husband said,
"If I painted that,
No one would believe it."
But we believe it, Lord.
We SAW it!

Just our luck!

Lord, You Are Everywhere

I find You
In the green hills,
In a drop of dew,
In the sea gull's wing,
In the grain of sand.

But today, dear Lord,
I see Your work
In my brand new grandson's
Tiny hand.

Thy Wonders

Lord,
You make some mornings
So beautiful,
It's a wonder
We report to work at all.

We drive down Broadway
In air crisp as cornflakes,
Past houses with their morning faces
Smiling in the sun,
Past children in red jackets
Skipping to school.

The sky is as blue
As only You can paint it,
And Mount Baldy sparkles with snow
So clear it seems
Almost within reach.

We are so overwhelmed
With Your perfection
We carry it into our jobs
With a glow that lasts
Almost until noon.

Lord,
Help us to maintain this joy
In Your magnificence,
Apart from any weather,
Beyond surface pleasure
In the obvious.
Help us to spin it out
All the way home again,
Through five o'clock smog,
And all through
Our lives.

Under the Stars

Lord,
I am by nature
An outdoor person.
Seas and mountains lure me
As moth to the flame.
Stretches of desert
Nourish me,
Green hills
Refresh me,
And a sunset
From our Pacific shore
Overwhelms me.

You do not speak to me
From the burning bush,
Or the pillar of cloud,
But You I hear
In all these wondrous settings,
Loud and clear.

Lord,
I am more than thankful
For the housing and shelter
You so amply provide.
I know You are there, too.
But Lord,
I cannot help it.
I feel closer to You
Outside!

On the Way to the Bank

Those men
On the road to Emmaus,
How could they not
Have recognized You?
Were they so preoccupied
With their troubles
That they were blind
To Your shining presence?
How could they?

Just the way
I rush along Fourth Street,
Head down, mind cluttered
With daily trivia,
Forgetting that
You walk beside me!

Guideline

There are winter nights
When I grope my way home
From a late meeting
Along foggy streets,
Hugging that white line
On the pavement
As my only guide.

Lord,
How often You have been
My white line
Through the fogs
Of my life.

44

World Population

From the census bureau
Have come the latest statistics,
The staggering number
Of people across the land,
The mind-boggling figures
Too great to understand.

But Lord,
What is more awesome,
More breath-stopping,
Is that from all corners,
All nations the same,
You call each one of us
By name!

Storm Damage

The rains last night
Brought ruin
To the neighborhood.
Flooded intersections,
Mud slides across roads,
Lines down,
No power, no phone.
We were cut off,
Alone.

We sat in the darkness
And felt the stillness
Of isolation.

Thank You, Lord,
For that strong line to You
That is never down
And the Light
That never goes out.

46

Bank Day

With my unerring skill
I have once again
Chosen the line
Which moves at a snail's pace
To the teller's window.

How merciful, Lord,
That we never have to
Wait in line
For You.

7 A.M. Summertime

This exquisite morning
Is one for the jewel box.
I take my mug of coffee
And my devotions
Out to the patio,
Where the dew lies beaded
Along the ferns
And glistens like crystal
Among the red begonias.
Somewhere in the eaves
A mourning dove
Calls softly
Into the early quiet.

Later, I must come in
And dress for the business day,
But these few moments
With You, Lord,
Are the jewels I will wear
All day.

And All Around My Soul

New Directions

There are days, Lord,
When I spend too much time
On soul-searching,
On in-dwelling
And indecision.

I have let
My insights narrow
Into tunnel vision,
Unable to see
Beyond myself.

I think too much
About the me of things,
And must try harder
To focus on
The Thee of things!

I Am His Own

There are days, Lord,
When I feel absolutely useless,
A scrap of insignificant material,
A remnant left over
From some discarded bolt,
A pattern never to be reordered
Because it wasn't a winner.

Then You remind me
With a gentle jolt
That I am a product
Of Your creation,
And in Your hand
Lies perfection,
That by Your own design
You have placed me
Only slightly lower
Than the angels,
And to You
I am important.

How could I ever forget, Lord,
That with You
I can always be
A winner?

You Did It Again!

How patiently, Lord,
When I fall on my face,
You pick me up,
Brush me off,
And restore me to grace.

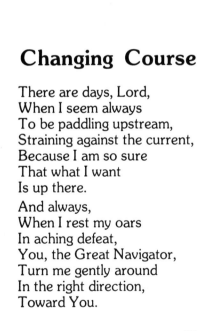

Changing Course

There are days, Lord,
When I seem always
To be paddling upstream,
Straining against the current,
Because I am so sure
That what I want
Is up there.

And always,
When I rest my oars
In aching defeat,
You, the Great Navigator,
Turn me gently around
In the right direction,
Toward You.

One Master

Lord,
I seem to wear
So many different hats,
Trying to be all things
To those around me:

Wife, mother,
Grandmother,
Friend, neighbor,
Confidante, companion,
Co-worker, classmate.

Sometimes I feel
So splintered,
So fragmented,
I am not sure
Just what I am
Or who.

Lord,
Help me to pull
My act together,
To stop questioning whether
I am this, or that.
Remind me I am
Answerable only
To You.

Inner Image

When I look
In the mirror, Lord,
I am not greatly impressed
With me.

But living so close to You
Has made me FEEL
Beautiful.

I hope that is what
Others see.

Go and Tell

Lord,
I love belonging
To Your army of Christian soldiers,
Marching onward.

But Lord,
I have never been one
To lead a parade,
To beat the loud drum
Or shout the anthem.

Does it bother You, Lord,
That some of us
Pledge our faith quietly?
If we testify to
Love and thanks,
Just by keeping
In step with the ranks?

Lord,
I think I know why
You are silent.

Promise

It's all there, Lord.
Spelled out for us,
Plain as day.
Every *i* dotted,
Every *t* crossed,
Between every line
Of the Scriptures,
Your eternal promise . . .
"I am with you always."

Why do *we* so often
Forget to read
The fine print?

Birthday

Lord,
You have let me come
This far
Without too many disasters,
With more happiness
Than sorrow,
With more sky-blue days
Than cloudy,
And untold blessings.
I promise not to worry
About tomorrow,
Because I know You will stay
Right beside me
The rest of the way.

Cameo Role

Sometimes, Lord,
I feel so ordinary,
So dull and uninteresting.
My friends jet across oceans
While I trundle to the shopping mall
To do the marketing.
I'll never do anything
To make the *Guinness Book of World Records*.
My exposure to excitement
Is limited to the six o'clock news.

What do You see in me, Lord,
That You can possibly use?

Forgive me, Lord,
For I know in my heart,
Whatever Your plan
I have a part.

For Better or for Worse

Lord,
You have given me
Such a stalwart man!
All these years
He has been
My fortress,
My ballast,
My wailing wall.

He has steadied me,
Supported me,
And most of all,
Loved me.

I am sure
It is only by
Your divine tact
He never seems to suspect
He is too good for me!

Account Payable

Lord,
For all the services
You have rendered me
Throughout my life,
As Advisor,
Comforter,
Counselor,
Forgiver,
Healer,
Listener,
Protector,
Teacher,
You have never once
Sent me a bill.

Only a statement stamped
"Paid in Advance."

Conceit

I must confess that I blossom
Beneath compliments,
That a pat on the back
For a job well done
Does incredible things
For my ego.

Dear Lord,
Help me to hang on
To humility,
Never, never forgetting
That all praise
Belongs to You!

Handywoman

Lord,
I think I am finally learning
That solving my problems
Will never be a
Do-it-yourself project.

It takes two:
Me and You.

Directional Signal

Lord,
Sometimes my prayers
Spill all over the map,
Take no steady route,
Zigzag back and forth.
My compass needle
Spins crazily,
Never still

Until

I remember to say:
"Thy will."

Relapse

In spite of all
My good resolutions,
In spite of my stout insistence
And virtuous protestations
That I have turned my life
Completely over to You,
I have failed again, Lord!

My pulse races
And jumps the track.
I am having an
Anxiety attack!
My fortresses have weakened,
My walls have cracked,
My foundations
Are not steady.

Lord, reach down
And hold my hand once more
Until I am ready.

Lord, You Are So Patient

How often You must smile
At my feeble attempts
To run my own life,
When I make a shambles
Of daily affairs,
Muddling through,
Sifting, sorting,
Making decisions
About what to do.

How merciful, Lord,
That You still smile
When I smugly take credit
For having reached a goal,
When all the while,
You were in control!

Letting Go

Lord,
If I have learned
Anything at all,
It is that I must let go
Of the reins to my life
And let You
Have the lead.

Time and again,
While praying to You,
I would refuse to surrender
My own will,
Insisting I could
Handle the situation
With just a little help
From You.

Lord, I apologize
For taking so long to learn
That my need
Is not to lead,
But to follow!

Reconciliation

Until the doorbell rang
I had not known
What to say
Or what to do
In this confrontation.

We had agreed
To forgive and forget,
To meet again
And start over,
But the moment was here
And I was mute with fear.

Oh! Thank You, Lord,
For that last-minute rescue,
Showing me
For laying old hurts to rest,
A hug is best!

Lord, You Are My Favorite Editor

I, who love the polished phrase,
Who take pride in the
Neatly turned word
And crisp articulation,
Must plead guilty
To submitting prayers to You
That are often
Poorly expressed,
Even ungrammatical,
And in times of stress
Bordering on incoherence.

Yet You never once
Correct my punctuation,
Criticize my style,
Blue-pencil a single word,
Or offer marketing tips.
What's more,
You never send
Rejection slips!

Food for My Soul

Feasting on Your Word, Lord,
Is so safe.
We need never
Study the label
For harmful ingredients,
Nor worry about
Artificial coloring,
Chemical preservatives
Or cancer-producing
Additives.

There is only pure,
Unadulterated
Truth.

Bygones

Lord,
I am guilty of forgiving
But not forgetting.

The ugly picture
Stays in my mind
With photographic clarity.
The image refuses
To fade or blur
With time.
I cannot seem
To detach it
From my memory.

Lord,
Help me to destroy
The negative
So there can never be
Another print.

Valley

There was a period
In my life
When I had sunk so low
Into the depths of despair
As to need
Intravenous feedings
Of Your Word
To bring me out.

Lord,
May I never again
Let Your life-sustaining formula
Become diluted
With doubt.

Poor Me!

There are days, Lord,
When I feel abused
And put upon.
Too much expected of me,
Taken for granted
By my family,
Ill used, depressed.

Oh! Lord,
How much more often
Have I treated You
In this very way,
And You never
Protest.

Lesson

I once thought that
Acquiring true spiritual peace
Would require a long,
Demanding apprenticeship
Of relentless discipline,
Sterile self-denial,
Rigid adherence
To narrow paths.
Now I know
That You have made it
As simple
As ABC:

One gentle imperative,
"Follow Me!"

Viewpoint

Lord,
This much I know:

Since I shifted focus
From me to YOU,
Nothing is the same.
Everything is new.

My Week

Sunday

Thank You, Lord,
For the Sabbath,
That precious day
Of worship and adoration.

Thank You
For the comfort
Of liturgy,
The blessings
Of the sacraments,
The restoration.

Thank You
For dedicated pastors
And thoughtful sermons,
For organ music
Ringing from Gothic peak.

Oh! Thank You, Lord,
For the Sabbath,
That priceless structure
On which I build
My week.

Monday

On laundry day,
The spot remover
With which I spray
The stains on our clothing
Works for awhile.
It is not guaranteed
To last forever.

But, Lord,
You washed away
All my stains,
With a lifetime guarantee
At Calvary.

Tuesday

This Bible class for seniors
Reflects Your special grace;
It falls on every snowy head
And glows from every face.
Ignoring small infirmities,
With here and there a cane,
Your faithful students gather,
Come storms or wind or rain.

Methuselah's great age would pale
Beside our totaled years,
We've had our share of living,
Of tragedies and tears.
Still we come together
Eager and smiling, when
The patient pastor leads us
Each Tuesday morn at ten.

Wednesday

(At Lutheran Bible Translators)

This is my day
To volunteer.
My privilege, really,
To join these workers
At the home office,
To stuff envelopes,
To fold or seal,
Staple, stamp,
Count, sift, sort.
No job too small
Or tedious.

Anything to help
Those servants in the field,
Whose selfless dedication
Brings Your Word
To every nation.

Thursday

This lovely young woman
With whom I am
Having lunch today
Sets such an
Inspiring example
Of spiritual strength.

I happen to know
Her steely endurance
Was forged in the fires
Of tribulation.
Yet she glows with
The inner radiation
Of Your grace.

Forgive my maternal pride, Lord,
In this beautiful blend
Of daughter
And friend.

Friday

When I feel breathless
And under pressure,
When I complain about
Too much to do

In this
Drip-dry,
No-iron,
Microwave,
Freeze-dried,
Instant mix,
Miniseries,
Digitalized,
Computerized
Fast lane
World

Please remind me
To stop the clock
And spend time
With You.

Saturday

(Company Coming)

Lord,
I have no trouble
Setting my priorities.
You come first,
For a fact!

Why, then, do I
Worry about
A crooked lampshade
Or magazines
Not neatly stacked?

Lord,
In Your graciousness,
Forgive my pettiness.

Finals

Lord, If You gave me
A report card
I wonder how
You would grade.

Mostly C's and D's,
An occasional E
I'm afraid.

But give me an A
For trying, Lord,
And from the foot
Of the class
Hear my voice in fervent thanks
That You have made it possible
For me to pass.